Plant Profile

Plant Name: _____

Date Planted: _____

Date Purchase: _____

Purchase at: _____

Price: _____

Rate: ☆ ☆ ☆ ☆ ☆

STARTED FROM

- ○ Seed
- ○ Transplant
- ○ Cutting
- ○ Bulb

- ○ Vegetable
- ○ Herb
- ○ Fruit

- ○ Flower
- ○ Tree

- ○ Annual
- ○ Perennial
- ○ Biennial

SUNLIGHT   WATER

Supplier: _____

Cost: _____

Date Sown: _____

Date Germinated: _____

Date Planted Out: _____

Date Bloomed: _____

Fertilizer / Soil Amendment: _____

Pests / Weeds Control: _____

Date of First Harvest: _____

PLANTING INSTRUCTIONS	CARE INSTRUCTIONS	FERTILIZERS & EQUIPMENT

GARDENING LOG BOOK

BELONGS TO

DATE	EVENT

MAKY
PUBLISHING

Greetings!

I am Martin, the founder of Maky Publishing, and I'm excited to share the story behind our company. As a proud father, husband, gardener, and graphic designer, I juggle many roles. But my passion for creating beautiful and practical books has always remained strong.

The photo below shows me and **my family, my greatest source of inspiration**. My wife is an incredible writer who has penned a popular book for new moms and a guide for parents, single parents, teachers, and anyone who wants to help children handle conflicts. We have two amazing children who always lend their creative touch to our projects. We love nature, animals, gardening, and traveling and strive to bring these passions to life through our work.

We're reaching out to you, our dear readers, for your valuable feedback. Your opinion matters to us, and we want to ensure that our books are beautiful but also practical and inspiring.

To leave feedback, scan this QR code and share your honest opinion on Amazon.

Scan this code or visit our website to claim your prize.

www.makypublishing.com

At Maky Publishing, we believe in creating a community of passionate readers and writers who support and inspire each other. Your feedback helps us improve, and we're committed to creating books you'll love.

**Thank you for being a part of our journey.
We look forward to hearing from you soon!**

Warm regards,

MARTIN AND MARTHA FOSTER
Founders of Maky Publishing

Year at Glance

January	February	March

April	May	June

July	August	September

October	November	December

Seasonal Garden Goals

Spring

- ○ _____
- ○ _____
- ○ _____
- ○ _____
- ○ _____
- ○ _____
- ○ _____
- ○ _____
- ○ _____
- ○ _____
- ○ _____
- ○ _____
- ○ _____
- ○ _____

Summer

- ○ _____
- ○ _____
- ○ _____
- ○ _____
- ○ _____
- ○ _____
- ○ _____
- ○ _____
- ○ _____
- ○ _____
- ○ _____
- ○ _____
- ○ _____
- ○ _____

Fall

- ○ _____
- ○ _____
- ○ _____
- ○ _____
- ○ _____
- ○ _____
- ○ _____
- ○ _____
- ○ _____
- ○ _____
- ○ _____
- ○ _____
- ○ _____

Winter

- ○ _____
- ○ _____
- ○ _____
- ○ _____
- ○ _____
- ○ _____
- ○ _____
- ○ _____
- ○ _____
- ○ _____
- ○ _____
- ○ _____
- ○ _____

Garden Layout

Note :

Garden Layout

Note :

Supplier Info

Supplier Name	Address	Contact Number	Email	Notes

Monthly Planner

January

Sunday	Monday	Tuesday	Wednesday	Thursday	Friday	Saturday

Note :

To-Do List

- ○ _____
- ○ _____
- ○ _____
- ○ _____
- ○ _____
- ○ _____
- ○ _____
- ○ _____
- ○ _____
- ○ _____
- ○ _____
- ○ _____
- ○ _____
- ○ _____
- ○ _____
- ○ _____
- ○ _____
- ○ _____
- ○ _____
- ○ _____
- ○ _____
- ○ _____
- ○ _____
- ○ _____
- ○ _____
- ○ _____
- ○ _____
- ○ _____
- ○ _____

- ○ _____
- ○ _____
- ○ _____
- ○ _____
- ○ _____
- ○ _____
- ○ _____
- ○ _____
- ○ _____
- ○ _____
- ○ _____
- ○ _____
- ○ _____
- ○ _____
- ○ _____
- ○ _____
- ○ _____
- ○ _____
- ○ _____
- ○ _____
- ○ _____
- ○ _____
- ○ _____
- ○ _____
- ○ _____
- ○ _____
- ○ _____
- ○ _____

Sow / Plant

_____   _____
_____   _____
_____   _____
_____   _____
_____   _____
_____   _____
_____   _____
_____   _____
_____   _____
_____   _____
_____   _____
_____   _____
_____   _____
_____   _____
_____   _____
_____   _____
_____   _____
_____   _____

Note :

Shopping List

_____
_____
_____
_____
_____
_____
_____
_____
_____
_____
_____
_____
_____
_____
_____
_____
_____
_____

Note :

Monthly Planner

February

Sunday	Monday	Tuesday	Wednesday	Thursday	Friday	Saturday

Note :

To-Do List

Sow / Plant

_____   _____
_____   _____
_____   _____
_____   _____
_____   _____
_____   _____
_____   _____
_____   _____
_____   _____
_____   _____
_____   _____
_____   _____
_____   _____
_____   _____
_____   _____
_____   _____
_____   _____
_____   _____
_____   _____

Note :

Shopping List

Note :

Monthly Planner

March

Sunday	Monday	Tuesday	Wednesday	Thursday	Friday	Saturday

Note :

To-Do List

○ _____
○ _____
○ _____
○ _____
○ _____
○ _____
○ _____
○ _____
○ _____
○ _____
○ _____
○ _____
○ _____
○ _____
○ _____
○ _____
○ _____
○ _____
○ _____
○ _____
○ _____
○ _____
○ _____
○ _____
○ _____
○ _____
○ _____
○ _____
○ _____

○ _____
○ _____
○ _____
○ _____
○ _____
○ _____
○ _____
○ _____
○ _____
○ _____
○ _____
○ _____
○ _____
○ _____
○ _____
○ _____
○ _____
○ _____
○ _____
○ _____
○ _____
○ _____
○ _____
○ _____
○ _____
○ _____
○ _____
○ _____
○ _____

Sow / Plant

Note :

Shopping List

_____   _____
_____   _____
_____   _____
_____   _____
_____   _____
_____   _____
_____   _____
_____   _____
_____   _____
_____   _____
_____   _____
_____   _____
_____   _____
_____   _____
_____   _____
_____   _____
_____   _____

Note :

Monthly Planner

April

Sunday	Monday	Tuesday	Wednesday	Thursday	Friday	Saturday

Note :

To-Do List

○ _____
○ _____
○ _____
○ _____
○ _____
○ _____
○ _____
○ _____
○ _____
○ _____
○ _____
○ _____
○ _____
○ _____
○ _____
○ _____
○ _____
○ _____
○ _____
○ _____
○ _____
○ _____
○ _____
○ _____
○ _____
○ _____
○ _____
○ _____
○ _____
○ _____

○ _____
○ _____
○ _____
○ _____
○ _____
○ _____
○ _____
○ _____
○ _____
○ _____
○ _____
○ _____
○ _____
○ _____
○ _____
○ _____
○ _____
○ _____
○ _____
○ _____
○ _____
○ _____
○ _____
○ _____
○ _____
○ _____
○ _____
○ _____
○ _____
○ _____

Sow / Plant

_____   _____
_____   _____
_____   _____
_____   _____
_____   _____
_____   _____
_____   _____
_____   _____
_____   _____
_____   _____
_____   _____
_____   _____
_____   _____
_____   _____
_____   _____
_____   _____
_____   _____
_____   _____

Note :

Shopping List

Note :

Monthly Planner

May

Sunday	Monday	Tuesday	Wednesday	Thursday	Friday	Saturday

Note :

To-Do List

○ _____
○ _____
○ _____
○ _____
○ _____
○ _____
○ _____
○ _____
○ _____
○ _____
○ _____
○ _____
○ _____
○ _____
○ _____
○ _____
○ _____
○ _____
○ _____
○ _____
○ _____
○ _____
○ _____
○ _____
○ _____
○ _____
○ _____
○ _____
○ _____
○ _____

○ _____
○ _____
○ _____
○ _____
○ _____
○ _____
○ _____
○ _____
○ _____
○ _____
○ _____
○ _____
○ _____
○ _____
○ _____
○ _____
○ _____
○ _____
○ _____
○ _____
○ _____
○ _____
○ _____
○ _____
○ _____
○ _____
○ _____
○ _____
○ _____
○ _____

Sow / Plant

_____

_____

_____

_____

_____

_____

_____

_____

_____

_____

_____

_____

_____

_____

_____

_____

_____

_____

_____

Note :

Shopping List

Monthly Planner

June

Sunday	Monday	Tuesday	Wednesday	Thursday	Friday	Saturday

Note :

To-Do List

○ _____   ○ _____
○ _____   ○ _____
○ _____   ○ _____
○ _____   ○ _____
○ _____   ○ _____
○ _____   ○ _____
○ _____   ○ _____
○ _____   ○ _____
○ _____   ○ _____
○ _____   ○ _____
○ _____   ○ _____
○ _____   ○ _____
○ _____   ○ _____
○ _____   ○ _____
○ _____   ○ _____
○ _____   ○ _____
○ _____   ○ _____
○ _____   ○ _____
○ _____   ○ _____
○ _____   ○ _____
○ _____   ○ _____
○ _____   ○ _____
○ _____   ○ _____
○ _____   ○ _____
○ _____   ○ _____
○ _____   ○ _____
○ _____   ○ _____
○ _____   ○ _____
○ _____   ○ _____
○ _____   ○ _____
○ _____   ○ _____

Sow / Plant

_____   _____
_____   _____
_____   _____
_____   _____
_____   _____
_____   _____
_____   _____
_____   _____
_____   _____
_____   _____
_____   _____
_____   _____
_____   _____
_____   _____
_____   _____
_____   _____
_____   _____
_____   _____
_____   _____
_____   _____
_____   _____

Note :

Shopping List

_____ | _____
_____ | _____
_____ | _____
_____ | _____
_____ | _____
_____ | _____
_____ | _____
_____ | _____
_____ | _____
_____ | _____
_____ | _____
_____ | _____
_____ | _____
_____ | _____
_____ | _____
_____ | _____
_____ | _____
_____ | _____
_____ | _____

Note :

Monthly Planner

July

Sunday	Monday	Tuesday	Wednesday	Thursday	Friday	Saturday

Note :

To-Do List

○ _____   ○ _____
○ _____   ○ _____
○ _____   ○ _____
○ _____   ○ _____
○ _____   ○ _____
○ _____   ○ _____
○ _____   ○ _____
○ _____   ○ _____
○ _____   ○ _____
○ _____   ○ _____
○ _____   ○ _____
○ _____   ○ _____
○ _____   ○ _____
○ _____   ○ _____
○ _____   ○ _____
○ _____   ○ _____
○ _____   ○ _____
○ _____   ○ _____
○ _____   ○ _____
○ _____   ○ _____
○ _____   ○ _____
○ _____   ○ _____
○ _____   ○ _____
○ _____   ○ _____
○ _____   ○ _____
○ _____   ○ _____
○ _____   ○ _____
○ _____   ○ _____
○ _____   ○ _____
○ _____   ○ _____

Sow / Plant

_____   _____
_____   _____
_____   _____
_____   _____
_____   _____
_____   _____
_____   _____
_____   _____
_____   _____
_____   _____
_____   _____
_____   _____
_____   _____
_____   _____
_____   _____
_____   _____
_____   _____
_____   _____
_____   _____
_____   _____
_____   _____
_____   _____

Note :

Shopping List

Note :

Monthly Planner

August

Sunday	Monday	Tuesday	Wednesday	Thursday	Friday	Saturday

Note :

To-Do List

○ _____
○ _____
○ _____
○ _____
○ _____
○ _____
○ _____
○ _____
○ _____
○ _____
○ _____
○ _____
○ _____
○ _____
○ _____
○ _____
○ _____
○ _____
○ _____
○ _____
○ _____
○ _____
○ _____
○ _____
○ _____
○ _____
○ _____
○ _____
○ _____
○ _____

○ _____
○ _____
○ _____
○ _____
○ _____
○ _____
○ _____
○ _____
○ _____
○ _____
○ _____
○ _____
○ _____
○ _____
○ _____
○ _____
○ _____
○ _____
○ _____
○ _____
○ _____
○ _____
○ _____
○ _____
○ _____
○ _____
○ _____
○ _____
○ _____
○ _____

Sow / Plant

_____   _____
_____   _____
_____   _____
_____   _____
_____   _____
_____   _____
_____   _____
_____   _____
_____   _____
_____   _____
_____   _____
_____   _____
_____   _____
_____   _____
_____   _____
_____   _____
_____   _____
_____   _____

Note :

Shopping List

_____ _____
_____ _____
_____ _____
_____ _____
_____ _____
_____ _____
_____ _____
_____ _____
_____ _____
_____ _____
_____ _____
_____ _____
_____ _____
_____ _____
_____ _____
_____ _____
_____ _____

Note :

Monthly Planner

September

Sunday	Monday	Tuesday	Wednesday	Thursday	Friday	Saturday

Note :

To-Do List

Sow / Plant

Note :

Shopping List

_____   _____
_____   _____
_____   _____
_____   _____
_____   _____
_____   _____
_____   _____
_____   _____
_____   _____
_____   _____
_____   _____
_____   _____
_____   _____
_____   _____
_____   _____
_____   _____
_____   _____
_____   _____

Note :

Monthly Planner

October

Sunday	Monday	Tuesday	Wednesday	Thursday	Friday	Saturday

Note :

To-Do List

Sow / Plant

Shopping List

_____ _____
_____ _____
_____ _____
_____ _____
_____ _____
_____ _____
_____ _____
_____ _____
_____ _____
_____ _____
_____ _____
_____ _____
_____ _____
_____ _____
_____ _____
_____ _____
_____ _____
_____ _____
_____ _____

Note :

Monthly Planner

November

Sunday	Monday	Tuesday	Wednesday	Thursday	Friday	Saturday

Note :

To-Do List

Sow / Plant

Note :

Shopping List

_____   _____
_____   _____
_____   _____
_____   _____
_____   _____
_____   _____
_____   _____
_____   _____
_____   _____
_____   _____
_____   _____
_____   _____
_____   _____
_____   _____
_____   _____
_____   _____
_____   _____
_____   _____
_____   _____

Note :

Monthly Planner

December

Sunday	Monday	Tuesday	Wednesday	Thursday	Friday	Saturday

Note :

To-Do List

Sow / Plant

Note :

Shopping List

_____   _____
_____   _____
_____   _____
_____   _____
_____   _____
_____   _____
_____   _____
_____   _____
_____   _____
_____   _____
_____   _____
_____   _____
_____   _____
_____   _____
_____   _____
_____   _____
_____   _____

Note :

Plant Profile

Plant Name:_____

Date Planted: _____

Date Purchase: _____

Purchase at: _____

Price:_____

Rate: ☆ ☆ ☆ ☆ ☆

STARTED FROM	PLANT TYPE		LIFE CYCLE	SUNLIGHT	WATER
○ Seed	○ Vegatable	○ Flower	○ Annual		
○ Transplant	○ Shrub	○ Tree	○ Biennial		
○ Cutting	○ Herb		○ Perennial		
○ Bulb	○ Fruit				

Supplier: _____

Cost: _____

Date Sown: _____

Date Germinated: _____

Date Planted Out:_____

Date Bloomed: _____

Fertilizer / Soil Amendment:_____

Pests / Weeds Control:_____

Date of First Harvest:_____

PLANTING INSTRUCTIONS	CARE INSTRUCTIONS	FERTILIZERS & EQUIPMENT

DATE	EVENT

DATE HARVESTED	QUANTITY	WEIGHT

DATE HARVESTED	QUANTITY	WEIGHT

NOTES

Plant Profile

Plant Name:_____

Date Planted: _____

Date Purchase: _____

Purchase at: _____

Price: _____

Rate: ☆ ☆ ☆ ☆ ☆

STARTED FROM	PLANT TYPE		LIFE CYCLE	SUNLIGHT	WATER
○ Seed	○ Vegatable	○ Flower	○ Annual		
○ Transplant	○ Shrub	○ Tree	○ Biennial		
○ Cutting	○ Herb		○ Perennial		
○ Bulb	○ Fruit				

Supplier: _____   Date Bloomed: _____

Cost: _____   Fertilizer / Soil Amendment:_____

Date Sown: _____   Pests / Weeds Control:_____

Date Germinated: _____   Date of First Harvest:_____

Date Planted Out:_____

PLANTING INSTRUCTIONS	CARE INSTRUCTIONS	FERTILIZERS & EQUIPMENT

DATE	EVENT

DATE HARVESTED	QUANTITY	WEIGHT

DATE HARVESTED	QUANTITY	WEIGHT

NOTES

Plant Profile

Plant Name:_____

Date Planted: _____

Date Purchase: _____

Purchase at: _____

Price: _____

Rate: ☆ ☆ ☆ ☆ ☆

STARTED FROM	PLANT TYPE		LIFE CYCLE	SUNLIGHT	WATER
○ Seed	○ Vegatable	○ Flower	○ Annual		
○ Transplant	○ Shrub	○ Tree	○ Biennial		
○ Cutting	○ Herb		○ Perennial		
○ Bulb	○ Fruit				

Supplier: _____   Date Bloomed: _____

Cost: _____   Fertilizer / Soil Amendment:_____

Date Sown:_____   Pests / Weeds Control:_____

Date Germinated: _____   Date of First Harvest:_____

Date Planted Out: _____

PLANTING INSTRUCTIONS	CARE INSTRUCTIONS	FERTILIZERS & EQUIPMENT

DATE	EVENT

DATE HARVESTED	QUANTITY	WEIGHT

DATE HARVESTED	QUANTITY	WEIGHT

NOTES

_____
_____
_____
_____
_____
_____
_____
_____
_____
_____
_____
_____
_____
_____
_____
_____
_____
_____
_____
_____
_____
_____
_____
_____
_____
_____
_____
_____

Plant Profile

Plant Name: _____

Date Planted: _____

Date Purchase: _____

Purchase at: _____

Price: _____

Rate: ☆ ☆ ☆ ☆ ☆

STARTED FROM	PLANT TYPE		LIFE CYCLE	SUNLIGHT	WATER
○ Seed	○ Vegatable	○ Flower	○ Annual		
○ Transplant	○ Shrub	○ Tree	○ Biennial		
○ Cutting	○ Herb		○ Perennial		
○ Bulb	○ Fruit				

Supplier: _____

Cost: _____

Date Sown: _____

Date Germinated: _____

Date Planted Out: _____

Date Bloomed: _____

Fertilizer / Soil Amendment: _____

Pests / Weeds Control: _____

Date of First Harvest: _____

PLANTING INSTRUCTIONS	CARE INSTRUCTIONS	FERTILIZERS & EQUIPMENT

DATE	EVENT

DATE HARVESTED	QUANTITY	WEIGHT

DATE HARVESTED	QUANTITY	WEIGHT

NOTES

Plant Profile

Plant Name:_____

Date Planted: _____

Date Purchase: _____

Purchase at: _____

Price: _____

Rate: ☆ ☆ ☆ ☆ ☆

STARTED FROM	PLANT TYPE		LIFE CYCLE	SUNLIGHT	WATER
○ Seed	○ Vegatable	○ Flower	○ Annual		
○ Transplant	○ Shrub	○ Tree	○ Biennial		
○ Cutting	○ Herb		○ Perennial		
○ Bulb	○ Fruit				

Supplier: _____   Date Bloomed: _____

Cost:_____   Fertilizer / Soil Amendment:_____

Date Sown:_____   Pests / Weeds Control:_____

Date Germinated: _____   Date of First Harvest:_____

Date Planted Out:_____

PLANTING INSTRUCTIONS	CARE INSTRUCTIONS	FERTILIZERS & EQUIPMENT

DATE	EVENT

DATE HARVESTED	QUANTITY	WEIGHT

DATE HARVESTED	QUANTITY	WEIGHT

NOTES

Plant Profile

Plant Name:_____

Date Planted: _____

Date Purchase: _____

Purchase at: _____

Price: _____

Rate: ☆ ☆ ☆ ☆ ☆

STARTED FROM	PLANT TYPE		LIFE CYCLE	SUNLIGHT	WATER
○ Seed	○ Vegatable	○ Flower	○ Annual	○ ☁	○ 💧
○ Transplant	○ Shrub	○ Tree	○ Biennial	○ ⛅	○ 💧💧
○ Cutting	○ Herb		○ Perennial	○ ☀	○ 💧💧💧
○ Bulb	○ Fruit				

Supplier: _____

Cost: _____

Date Sown: _____

Date Germinated: _____

Date Planted Out: _____

Date Bloomed: _____

Fertilizer / Soil Amendment:_____

Pests / Weeds Control: _____

Date of First Harvest:_____

PLANTING INSTRUCTIONS	CARE INSTRUCTIONS	FERTILIZERS & EQUIPMENT

DATE	EVENT

DATE HARVESTED	QUANTITY	WEIGHT

DATE HARVESTED	QUANTITY	WEIGHT

NOTES

Plant Profile

Plant Name:_____

Date Planted: _____

Date Purchase: _____

Purchase at: _____

Price: _____

Rate: ☆ ☆ ☆ ☆ ☆

STARTED FROM	PLANT TYPE		LIFE CYCLE
○ Seed	○ Vegatable	○ Flower	○ Annual
○ Transplant	○ Shrub	○ Tree	○ Biennial
○ Cutting	○ Herb		○ Perennial
○ Bulb	○ Fruit		

SUNLIGHT   WATER

Supplier: _____

Cost: _____

Date Sown: _____

Date Germinated: _____

Date Planted Out: _____

Date Bloomed: _____

Fertilizer / Soil Amendment:_____

Pests / Weeds Control:_____

Date of First Harvest: _____

PLANTING INSTRUCTIONS	CARE INSTRUCTIONS	FERTILIZERS & EQUIPMENT

DATE	EVENT

DATE HARVESTED	QUANTITY	WEIGHT

DATE HARVESTED	QUANTITY	WEIGHT

NOTES

Plant Profile

Plant Name:_____

Date Planted: _____

Date Purchase: _____

Purchase at: _____

Price: _____

Rate: ☆ ☆ ☆ ☆ ☆

STARTED FROM	PLANT TYPE		LIFE CYCLE	SUNLIGHT	WATER
○ Seed	○ Vegatable	○ Flower	○ Annual		
○ Transplant	○ Shrub	○ Tree	○ Biennial		
○ Cutting	○ Herb		○ Perennial		
○ Bulb	○ Fruit				

Supplier: _____   Date Bloomed: _____

Cost: _____   Fertilizer / Soil Amendment:_____

Date Sown:_____   Pests / Weeds Control:_____

Date Germinated: _____   Date of First Harvest:_____

Date Planted Out:_____

PLANTING INSTRUCTIONS	CARE INSTRUCTIONS	FERTILIZERS & EQUIPMENT

DATE	EVENT

DATE HARVESTED	QUANTITY	WEIGHT

DATE HARVESTED	QUANTITY	WEIGHT

NOTES

Plant Profile

Plant Name:_____

Date Planted: _____

Date Purchase: _____

Purchase at: _____

Price: _____

Rate: ☆☆☆☆☆

STARTED FROM	PLANT TYPE		LIFE CYCLE	SUNLIGHT	WATER
○ Seed	○ Vegatable	○ Flower	○ Annual		
○ Transplant	○ Shrub	○ Tree	○ Biennial		
○ Cutting	○ Herb		○ Perennial		
○ Bulb	○ Fruit				

Supplier: _____   Date Bloomed: _____

Cost: _____   Fertilizer / Soil Amendment:_____

Date Sown: _____   Pests / Weeds Control:_____

Date Germinated: _____   Date of First Harvest:_____

Date Planted Out:_____

PLANTING INSTRUCTIONS	CARE INSTRUCTIONS	FERTILIZERS & EQUIPMENT

DATE	EVENT

DATE HARVESTED	QUANTITY	WEIGHT

DATE HARVESTED	QUANTITY	WEIGHT

NOTES

Plant Profile

Plant Name:_____

Date Planted: _____

Date Purchase: _____

Purchase at: _____

Price: _____

Rate: ☆ ☆ ☆ ☆ ☆

STARTED FROM	PLANT TYPE		LIFE CYCLE	SUNLIGHT	WATER
○ Seed	○ Vegatable	○ Flower	○ Annual	○ ☁	○ 💧
○ Transplant	○ Shrub	○ Tree	○ Biennial	○ ⛅	○ 💧💧
○ Cutting	○ Herb		○ Perennial	○ ☀	○ 💧💧💧
○ Bulb	○ Fruit				

Supplier: _____

Cost: _____

Date Sown: _____

Date Germinated: _____

Date Planted Out: _____

Date Bloomed: _____

Fertilizer / Soil Amendment:_____

Pests / Weeds Control: _____

Date of First Harvest:_____

PLANTING INSTRUCTIONS	CARE INSTRUCTIONS	FERTILIZERS & EQUIPMENT

DATE	EVENT

DATE HARVESTED	QUANTITY	WEIGHT

DATE HARVESTED	QUANTITY	WEIGHT

NOTES

Plant Profile

Plant Name:_____

Date Planted: _____

Date Purchase: _____

Purchase at: _____

Price: _____

Rate: ☆ ☆ ☆ ☆ ☆

STARTED FROM	PLANT TYPE		LIFE CYCLE	SUNLIGHT	WATER
○ Seed	○ Vegatable	○ Flower	○ Annual		
○ Transplant	○ Shrub	○ Tree	○ Biennial		
○ Cutting	○ Herb		○ Perennial		
○ Bulb	○ Fruit				

Supplier: _____   Date Bloomed: _____

Cost: _____   Fertilizer / Soil Amendment:_____

Date Sown:_____   Pests / Weeds Control:_____

Date Germinated: _____   Date of First Harvest:_____

Date Planted Out: _____

PLANTING INSTRUCTIONS	CARE INSTRUCTIONS	FERTILIZERS & EQUIPMENT

DATE	EVENT

DATE HARVESTED	QUANTITY	WEIGHT

DATE HARVESTED	QUANTITY	WEIGHT

NOTES

Plant Profile

Plant Name:_____

Date Planted: _____

Date Purchase: _____

Purchase at: _____

Price: _____

Rate: ☆☆☆☆☆

STARTED FROM	PLANT TYPE		LIFE CYCLE	SUNLIGHT	WATER
○ Seed	○ Vegatable	○ Flower	○ Annual	○ ☁	○ 💧
○ Transplant	○ Shrub	○ Tree	○ Biennial	○ ⛅	○ 💧💧
○ Cutting	○ Herb		○ Perennial	○ ☀	○ 💧💧💧
○ Bulb	○ Fruit				

Supplier: _____   Date Bloomed: _____

Cost: _____   Fertilizer / Soil Amendment:_____

Date Sown:_____   Pests / Weeds Control:_____

Date Germinated: _____   Date of First Harvest:_____

Date Planted Out: _____

PLANTING INSTRUCTIONS	CARE INSTRUCTIONS	FERTILIZERS & EQUIPMENT

DATE	EVENT

DATE HARVESTED	QUANTITY	WEIGHT

DATE HARVESTED	QUANTITY	WEIGHT

NOTES

Plant Profile

Plant Name:_____

Date Planted: _____

Date Purchase: _____

Purchase at: _____

Price: _____

Rate: ☆ ☆ ☆ ☆ ☆

STARTED FROM	PLANT TYPE		LIFE CYCLE	SUNLIGHT	WATER
○ Seed	○ Vegatable	○ Flower	○ Annual	○ ☁	○ 💧
○ Transplant	○ Shrub	○ Tree	○ Biennial	○ ⛅	○ 💧💧
○ Cutting	○ Herb		○ Perennial	○ ☀	○ 💧💧💧
○ Bulb	○ Fruit				

Supplier: _____   Date Bloomed: _____

Cost: _____   Fertilizer / Soil Amendment:_____

Date Sown:_____   Pests / Weeds Control:_____

Date Germinated: _____   Date of First Harvest:_____

Date Planted Out: _____

PLANTING INSTRUCTIONS	CARE INSTRUCTIONS	FERTILIZERS & EQUIPMENT

DATE	EVENT

DATE HARVESTED	QUANTITY	WEIGHT		DATE HARVESTED	QUANTITY	WEIGHT

NOTES

Plant Profile

Plant Name:_____

Date Planted: _____

Date Purchase: _____

Purchase at: _____

Price: _____

Rate: ☆ ☆ ☆ ☆ ☆

STARTED FROM	PLANT TYPE		LIFE CYCLE	SUNLIGHT	WATER
○ Seed	○ Vegatable	○ Flower	○ Annual		
○ Transplant	○ Shrub	○ Tree	○ Biennial		
○ Cutting	○ Herb		○ Perennial		
○ Bulb	○ Fruit				

Supplier: _____   Date Bloomed: _____

Cost: _____   Fertilizer / Soil Amendment:_____

Date Sown:_____   Pests / Weeds Control:_____

Date Germinated: _____   Date of First Harvest:_____

Date Planted Out: _____

PLANTING INSTRUCTIONS	CARE INSTRUCTIONS	FERTILIZERS & EQUIPMENT

DATE	EVENT

DATE HARVESTED	QUANTITY	WEIGHT

DATE HARVESTED	QUANTITY	WEIGHT

NOTES

Plant Profile

Plant Name:_____

Date Planted: _____

Date Purchase: _____

Purchase at: _____

Price: _____

Rate: ☆ ☆ ☆ ☆ ☆

STARTED FROM	PLANT TYPE		LIFE CYCLE	SUNLIGHT	WATER
○ Seed	○ Vegatable	○ Flower	○ Annual		
○ Transplant	○ Shrub	○ Tree	○ Biennial		
○ Cutting	○ Herb		○ Perennial		
○ Bulb	○ Fruit				

Supplier: _____   Date Bloomed: _____

Cost: _____   Fertilizer / Soil Amendment: _____

Date Sown: _____   Pests / Weeds Control: _____

Date Germinated: _____   Date of First Harvest: _____

Date Planted Out: _____

PLANTING INSTRUCTIONS	CARE INSTRUCTIONS	FERTILIZERS & EQUIPMENT

DATE	EVENT

DATE HARVESTED	QUANTITY	WEIGHT

DATE HARVESTED	QUANTITY	WEIGHT

NOTES

Plant Profile

Plant Name:_____

Date Planted: _____

Date Purchase: _____

Purchase at: _____

Price: _____

Rate: ☆☆☆☆☆

STARTED FROM	PLANT TYPE		LIFE CYCLE	SUNLIGHT	WATER
○ Seed	○ Vegatable	○ Flower	○ Annual		
○ Transplant	○ Shrub	○ Tree	○ Biennial		
○ Cutting	○ Herb		○ Perennial		
○ Bulb	○ Fruit				

Supplier: _____

Cost: _____

Date Sown: _____

Date Germinated: _____

Date Planted Out: _____

Date Bloomed: _____

Fertilizer / Soil Amendment:_____

Pests / Weeds Control:_____

Date of First Harvest:_____

PLANTING INSTRUCTIONS	CARE INSTRUCTIONS	FERTILIZERS & EQUIPMENT

DATE	EVENT

DATE HARVESTED	QUANTITY	WEIGHT

DATE HARVESTED	QUANTITY	WEIGHT

NOTES

Plant Profile

Plant Name:_____

Date Planted: _____

Date Purchase: _____

Purchase at: _____

Price: _____

Rate: ☆ ☆ ☆ ☆ ☆

STARTED FROM	PLANT TYPE		LIFE CYCLE	SUNLIGHT	WATER
○ Seed	○ Vegatable	○ Flower	○ Annual		
○ Transplant	○ Shrub	○ Tree	○ Biennial		
○ Cutting	○ Herb		○ Perennial		
○ Bulb	○ Fruit				

Supplier: _____

Cost: _____

Date Sown:_____

Date Germinated: _____

Date Planted Out:_____

Date Bloomed: _____

Fertilizer / Soil Amendment:_____

Pests / Weeds Control: _____

Date of First Harvest:_____

PLANTING INSTRUCTIONS	CARE INSTRUCTIONS	FERTILIZERS & EQUIPMENT

DATE	EVENT

DATE HARVESTED	QUANTITY	WEIGHT

DATE HARVESTED	QUANTITY	WEIGHT

NOTES

Plant Profile

Plant Name:_____

Date Planted: _____

Date Purchase: _____

Purchase at: _____

Price: _____

Rate: ☆ ☆ ☆ ☆ ☆

STARTED FROM	PLANT TYPE		LIFE CYCLE	SUNLIGHT	WATER
○ Seed	○ Vegatable	○ Flower	○ Annual		
○ Transplant	○ Shrub	○ Tree	○ Biennial		
○ Cutting	○ Herb		○ Perennial		
○ Bulb	○ Fruit				

Supplier: _____

Cost: _____

Date Sown: _____

Date Germinated: _____

Date Planted Out: _____

Date Bloomed: _____

Fertilizer / Soil Amendment:_____

Pests / Weeds Control: _____

Date of First Harvest: _____

PLANTING INSTRUCTIONS	CARE INSTRUCTIONS	FERTILIZERS & EQUIPMENT

DATE	EVENT

DATE HARVESTED	QUANTITY	WEIGHT

DATE HARVESTED	QUANTITY	WEIGHT

NOTES

Plant Profile

Plant Name:_____

Date Planted: _____

Date Purchase: _____

Purchase at: _____

Price: _____

Rate: ☆ ☆ ☆ ☆ ☆

STARTED FROM	PLANT TYPE		LIFE CYCLE	SUNLIGHT	WATER
○ Seed	○ Vegatable	○ Flower	○ Annual		
○ Transplant	○ Shrub	○ Tree	○ Biennial		
○ Cutting	○ Herb		○ Perennial		
○ Bulb	○ Fruit				

Supplier: _____   Date Bloomed: _____

Cost:_____   Fertilizer / Soil Amendment:_____

Date Sown:_____   Pests / Weeds Control:_____

Date Germinated: _____   Date of First Harvest:_____

Date Planted Out:_____

PLANTING INSTRUCTIONS	CARE INSTRUCTIONS	FERTILIZERS & EQUIPMENT

DATE	EVENT

DATE HARVESTED	QUANTITY	WEIGHT

DATE HARVESTED	QUANTITY	WEIGHT

NOTES

Plant Profile

Plant Name:_____

Date Planted: _____

Date Purchase: _____

Purchase at: _____

Price: _____

Rate: ☆ ☆ ☆ ☆ ☆

STARTED FROM	PLANT TYPE		LIFE CYCLE	SUNLIGHT	WATER
○ Seed	○ Vegatable	○ Flower	○ Annual		
○ Transplant	○ Shrub	○ Tree	○ Biennial		
○ Cutting	○ Herb		○ Perennial		
○ Bulb	○ Fruit				

Supplier: _____

Cost: _____

Date Sown: _____

Date Germinated: _____

Date Planted Out: _____

Date Bloomed: _____

Fertilizer / Soil Amendment:_____

Pests / Weeds Control:_____

Date of First Harvest:_____

PLANTING INSTRUCTIONS	CARE INSTRUCTIONS	FERTILIZERS & EQUIPMENT

DATE	EVENT

DATE HARVESTED	QUANTITY	WEIGHT

DATE HARVESTED	QUANTITY	WEIGHT

NOTES

Plant Profile

Plant Name:_____

Date Planted: _____

Date Purchase: _____

Purchase at: _____

Price: _____

Rate: ☆ ☆ ☆ ☆ ☆

STARTED FROM	PLANT TYPE		LIFE CYCLE	SUNLIGHT	WATER
○ Seed	○ Vegatable	○ Flower	○ Annual		
○ Transplant	○ Shrub	○ Tree	○ Biennial		
○ Cutting	○ Herb		○ Perennial		
○ Bulb	○ Fruit				

Supplier: _____   Date Bloomed: _____

Cost: _____   Fertilizer / Soil Amendment:_____

Date Sown:_____   Pests / Weeds Control:_____

Date Germinated: _____   Date of First Harvest:_____

Date Planted Out: _____

PLANTING INSTRUCTIONS	CARE INSTRUCTIONS	FERTILIZERS & EQUIPMENT

DATE	EVENT

DATE HARVESTED	QUANTITY	WEIGHT

DATE HARVESTED	QUANTITY	WEIGHT

NOTES

Plant Profile

Plant Name:_____

Date Planted: _____

Date Purchase: _____

Purchase at: _____

Price:_____

Rate: ☆☆☆☆☆

STARTED FROM	PLANT TYPE		LIFE CYCLE	SUNLIGHT	WATER
○ Seed	○ Vegatable	○ Flower	○ Annual		
○ Transplant	○ Shrub	○ Tree	○ Biennial		
○ Cutting	○ Herb		○ Perennial		
○ Bulb	○ Fruit				

Supplier: _____   Date Bloomed: _____

Cost: _____   Fertilizer / Soil Amendment:_____

Date Sown:_____   Pests / Weeds Control:_____

Date Germinated: _____   Date of First Harvest:_____

Date Planted Out: _____

PLANTING INSTRUCTIONS	CARE INSTRUCTIONS	FERTILIZERS & EQUIPMENT

DATE	EVENT

DATE HARVESTED	QUANTITY	WEIGHT

DATE HARVESTED	QUANTITY	WEIGHT

NOTES

Plant Profile

Plant Name:_____

Date Planted: _____

Date Purchase: _____

Purchase at: _____

Price: _____

Rate: ☆ ☆ ☆ ☆ ☆

STARTED FROM	PLANT TYPE		LIFE CYCLE	SUNLIGHT	WATER
○ Seed	○ Vegatable	○ Flower	○ Annual		
○ Transplant	○ Shrub	○ Tree	○ Biennial		
○ Cutting	○ Herb		○ Perennial		
○ Bulb	○ Fruit				

Supplier: _____

Cost: _____

Date Sown:_____

Date Germinated: _____

Date Planted Out:_____

Date Bloomed: _____

Fertilizer / Soil Amendment:_____

Pests / Weeds Control:_____

Date of First Harvest: _____

PLANTING INSTRUCTIONS	CARE INSTRUCTIONS	FERTILIZERS & EQUIPMENT

DATE	EVENT

DATE HARVESTED	QUANTITY	WEIGHT

DATE HARVESTED	QUANTITY	WEIGHT

NOTES

Plant Profile

Plant Name:_____

Date Planted: _____

Date Purchase: _____

Purchase at: _____

Price: _____

Rate: ☆ ☆ ☆ ☆ ☆

STARTED FROM	PLANT TYPE		LIFE CYCLE	SUNLIGHT	WATER
○ Seed	○ Vegatable	○ Flower	○ Annual	○	○
○ Transplant	○ Shrub	○ Tree	○ Biennial	○	○
○ Cutting	○ Herb		○ Perennial	○	○
○ Bulb	○ Fruit				

Supplier: _____   Date Bloomed: _____

Cost: _____   Fertilizer / Soil Amendment:_____

Date Sown:_____   Pests / Weeds Control:_____

Date Germinated: _____   Date of First Harvest:_____

Date Planted Out: _____

PLANTING INSTRUCTIONS	CARE INSTRUCTIONS	FERTILIZERS & EQUIPMENT

DATE	EVENT

DATE HARVESTED	QUANTITY	WEIGHT	DATE HARVESTED	QUANTITY	WEIGHT

NOTES

Plant Profile

Plant Name:_____

Date Planted: _____

Date Purchase: _____

Purchase at: _____

Price: _____

Rate: ☆ ☆ ☆ ☆ ☆

STARTED FROM	PLANT TYPE		LIFE CYCLE	SUNLIGHT	WATER
○ Seed	○ Vegatable	○ Flower	○ Annual		
○ Transplant	○ Shrub	○ Tree	○ Biennial		
○ Cutting	○ Herb		○ Perennial		
○ Bulb	○ Fruit				

Supplier: _____   Date Bloomed: _____

Cost: _____   Fertilizer / Soil Amendment:_____

Date Sown: _____   Pests / Weeds Control:_____

Date Germinated: _____   Date of First Harvest:_____

Date Planted Out: _____

PLANTING INSTRUCTIONS	CARE INSTRUCTIONS	FERTILIZERS & EQUIPMENT

DATE	EVENT

DATE HARVESTED	QUANTITY	WEIGHT

DATE HARVESTED	QUANTITY	WEIGHT

NOTES

Plant Profile

Plant Name:_____

Date Planted: _____

Date Purchase: _____

Purchase at: _____

Price: _____

Rate: ☆ ☆ ☆ ☆ ☆

STARTED FROM	PLANT TYPE		LIFE CYCLE	SUNLIGHT	WATER
○ Seed	○ Vegatable	○ Flower	○ Annual		
○ Transplant	○ Shrub	○ Tree	○ Biennial		
○ Cutting	○ Herb		○ Perennial		
○ Bulb	○ Fruit				

Supplier: _____

Cost:_____

Date Sown: _____

Date Germinated: _____

Date Planted Out: _____

Date Bloomed: _____

Fertilizer / Soil Amendment:_____

Pests / Weeds Control:_____

Date of First Harvest:_____

PLANTING INSTRUCTIONS	CARE INSTRUCTIONS	FERTILIZERS & EQUIPMENT

DATE	EVENT

DATE HARVESTED	QUANTITY	WEIGHT

DATE HARVESTED	QUANTITY	WEIGHT

NOTES

Plant Profile

Plant Name:_____

Date Planted: _____

Date Purchase: _____

Purchase at: _____

Price: _____

Rate: ☆ ☆ ☆ ☆ ☆

STARTED FROM	PLANT TYPE		LIFE CYCLE	SUNLIGHT	WATER
○ Seed	○ Vegatable	○ Flower	○ Annual		
○ Transplant	○ Shrub	○ Tree	○ Biennial		
○ Cutting	○ Herb		○ Perennial		
○ Bulb	○ Fruit				

Supplier: _____   Date Bloomed: _____

Cost: _____   Fertilizer / Soil Amendment:_____

Date Sown: _____   Pests / Weeds Control: _____

Date Germinated: _____   Date of First Harvest: _____

Date Planted Out: _____

PLANTING INSTRUCTIONS	CARE INSTRUCTIONS	FERTILIZERS & EQUIPMENT

DATE	EVENT

DATE HARVESTED	QUANTITY	WEIGHT

DATE HARVESTED	QUANTITY	WEIGHT

NOTES

Plant Profile

Plant Name:_____

Date Planted: _____

Date Purchase: _____

Purchase at: _____

Price: _____

Rate: ☆ ☆ ☆ ☆ ☆

STARTED FROM	PLANT TYPE		LIFE CYCLE	SUNLIGHT	WATER
○ Seed	○ Vegatable	○ Flower	○ Annual		
○ Transplant	○ Shrub	○ Tree	○ Biennial		
○ Cutting	○ Herb		○ Perennial		
○ Bulb	○ Fruit				

Supplier: _____ Date Bloomed: _____

Cost: _____ Fertilizer / Soil Amendment:_____

Date Sown: _____ Pests / Weeds Control:_____

Date Germinated: _____ Date of First Harvest:_____

Date Planted Out: _____

PLANTING INSTRUCTIONS	CARE INSTRUCTIONS	FERTILIZERS & EQUIPMENT

DATE	EVENT

DATE HARVESTED	QUANTITY	WEIGHT

DATE HARVESTED	QUANTITY	WEIGHT

NOTES

Plant Profile

Plant Name:_____

Date Planted: _____

Date Purchase: _____

Purchase at: _____

Price: _____

Rate: ☆☆☆☆☆

STARTED FROM	PLANT TYPE		LIFE CYCLE	SUNLIGHT	WATER
○ Seed	○ Vegatable	○ Flower	○ Annual		
○ Transplant	○ Shrub	○ Tree	○ Biennial		
○ Cutting	○ Herb		○ Perennial		
○ Bulb	○ Fruit				

Supplier: _____   Date Bloomed: _____

Cost: _____   Fertilizer / Soil Amendment:_____

Date Sown: _____   Pests / Weeds Control:_____

Date Germinated: _____   Date of First Harvest:_____

Date Planted Out:_____

PLANTING INSTRUCTIONS	CARE INSTRUCTIONS	FERTILIZERS & EQUIPMENT

DATE	EVENT

DATE HARVESTED	QUANTITY	WEIGHT

DATE HARVESTED	QUANTITY	WEIGHT

NOTES

Plant Profile

Plant Name:_____

Date Planted: _____

Date Purchase: _____

Purchase at: _____

Price: _____

Rate: ☆ ☆ ☆ ☆ ☆

STARTED FROM	PLANT TYPE		LIFE CYCLE	SUNLIGHT	WATER
○ Seed	○ Vegatable	○ Flower	○ Annual		
○ Transplant	○ Shrub	○ Tree	○ Biennial		
○ Cutting	○ Herb		○ Perennial		
○ Bulb	○ Fruit				

Supplier: _____   Date Bloomed: _____

Cost:_____   Fertilizer / Soil Amendment:_____

Date Sown: _____   Pests / Weeds Control:_____

Date Germinated: _____   Date of First Harvest:_____

Date Planted Out: _____

PLANTING INSTRUCTIONS	CARE INSTRUCTIONS	FERTILIZERS & EQUIPMENT

DATE	EVENT

DATE HARVESTED	QUANTITY	WEIGHT

DATE HARVESTED	QUANTITY	WEIGHT

NOTES

Plant Profile

Plant Name:_____

Date Planted: _____

Date Purchase: _____

Purchase at: _____

Price: _____

Rate: ☆ ☆ ☆ ☆ ☆

STARTED FROM	PLANT TYPE		LIFE CYCLE	SUNLIGHT	WATER
○ Seed	○ Vegatable	○ Flower	○ Annual		
○ Transplant	○ Shrub	○ Tree	○ Biennial		
○ Cutting	○ Herb		○ Perennial		
○ Bulb	○ Fruit				

Supplier: _____   Date Bloomed: _____

Cost: _____   Fertilizer / Soil Amendment:_____

Date Sown: _____   Pests / Weeds Control: _____

Date Germinated: _____   Date of First Harvest: _____

Date Planted Out: _____

PLANTING INSTRUCTIONS	CARE INSTRUCTIONS	FERTILIZERS & EQUIPMENT

DATE	EVENT

DATE HARVESTED	QUANTITY	WEIGHT

DATE HARVESTED	QUANTITY	WEIGHT

NOTES

Plant Profile

Plant Name:_____

Date Planted: _____

Date Purchase: _____

Purchase at: _____

Price: _____

Rate: ☆ ☆ ☆ ☆ ☆

STARTED FROM	PLANT TYPE		LIFE CYCLE	SUNLIGHT	WATER
○ Seed	○ Vegatable	○ Flower	○ Annual		
○ Transplant	○ Shrub	○ Tree	○ Biennial		
○ Cutting	○ Herb		○ Perennial		
○ Bulb	○ Fruit				

Supplier: _____ Date Bloomed: _____

Cost: _____ Fertilizer / Soil Amendment:_____

Date Sown:_____ Pests / Weeds Control:_____

Date Germinated: _____ Date of First Harvest: _____

Date Planted Out:_____

PLANTING INSTRUCTIONS	CARE INSTRUCTIONS	FERTILIZERS & EQUIPMENT

DATE	EVENT

DATE HARVESTED	QUANTITY	WEIGHT

DATE HARVESTED	QUANTITY	WEIGHT

NOTES

Plant Profile

Plant Name:_____

Date Planted: _____

Date Purchase: _____

Purchase at: _____

Price: _____

Rate: ☆ ☆ ☆ ☆ ☆

STARTED FROM	PLANT TYPE		LIFE CYCLE	SUNLIGHT	WATER
○ Seed	○ Vegatable	○ Flower	○ Annual		
○ Transplant	○ Shrub	○ Tree	○ Biennial		
○ Cutting	○ Herb		○ Perennial		
○ Bulb	○ Fruit				

Supplier: _____   Date Bloomed: _____

Cost:_____   Fertilizer / Soil Amendment:_____

Date Sown:_____   Pests / Weeds Control:_____

Date Germinated: _____   Date of First Harvest:_____

Date Planted Out:_____

PLANTING INSTRUCTIONS	CARE INSTRUCTIONS	FERTILIZERS & EQUIPMENT

DATE	EVENT

DATE HARVESTED	QUANTITY	WEIGHT

DATE HARVESTED	QUANTITY	WEIGHT

NOTES

Plant Profile

Plant Name:_____

Date Planted: _____

Date Purchase: _____

Purchase at: _____

Price: _____

Rate: ☆ ☆ ☆ ☆ ☆

STARTED FROM	PLANT TYPE		LIFE CYCLE	SUNLIGHT	WATER
○ Seed	○ Vegatable	○ Flower	○ Annual		
○ Transplant	○ Shrub	○ Tree	○ Biennial		
○ Cutting	○ Herb		○ Perennial		
○ Bulb	○ Fruit				

Supplier: _____   Date Bloomed: _____

Cost: _____   Fertilizer / Soil Amendment:_____

Date Sown:_____   Pests / Weeds Control: _____

Date Germinated: _____   Date of First Harvest:_____

Date Planted Out: _____

PLANTING INSTRUCTIONS	CARE INSTRUCTIONS	FERTILIZERS & EQUIPMENT

DATE	EVENT

DATE HARVESTED	QUANTITY	WEIGHT

DATE HARVESTED	QUANTITY	WEIGHT

NOTES

Plant Profile

Plant Name:_____

Date Planted: _____

Date Purchase: _____

Purchase at: _____

Price: _____

Rate: ☆ ☆ ☆ ☆ ☆

STARTED FROM	PLANT TYPE		LIFE CYCLE	SUNLIGHT	WATER
○ Seed	○ Vegatable	○ Flower	○ Annual		
○ Transplant	○ Shrub	○ Tree	○ Biennial		
○ Cutting	○ Herb		○ Perennial		
○ Bulb	○ Fruit				

Supplier: _____   Date Bloomed: _____

Cost: _____   Fertilizer / Soil Amendment:_____

Date Sown:_____   Pests / Weeds Control:_____

Date Germinated: _____   Date of First Harvest:_____

Date Planted Out:_____

PLANTING INSTRUCTIONS	CARE INSTRUCTIONS	FERTILIZERS & EQUIPMENT

DATE	EVENT

DATE HARVESTED	QUANTITY	WEIGHT

DATE HARVESTED	QUANTITY	WEIGHT

NOTES

Plant Profile

Plant Name:_____

Date Planted: _____

Date Purchase: _____

Purchase at: _____

Price:_____

Rate: ☆ ☆ ☆ ☆ ☆

STARTED FROM	PLANT TYPE		LIFE CYCLE	SUNLIGHT	WATER
○ Seed	○ Vegatable	○ Flower	○ Annual		
○ Transplant	○ Shrub	○ Tree	○ Biennial		
○ Cutting	○ Herb		○ Perennial		
○ Bulb	○ Fruit				

Supplier: _____

Cost: _____

Date Sown: _____

Date Germinated: _____

Date Planted Out: _____

Date Bloomed: _____

Fertilizer / Soil Amendment:_____

Pests / Weeds Control:_____

Date of First Harvest:_____

PLANTING INSTRUCTIONS	CARE INSTRUCTIONS	FERTILIZERS & EQUIPMENT

DATE	EVENT

DATE HARVESTED	QUANTITY	WEIGHT

DATE HARVESTED	QUANTITY	WEIGHT

NOTES

Plant Profile

Plant Name:_____

Date Planted: _____

Date Purchase: _____

Purchase at: _____

Price: _____

Rate: ☆ ☆ ☆ ☆ ☆

STARTED FROM	PLANT TYPE		LIFE CYCLE	SUNLIGHT	WATER
○ Seed	○ Vegatable	○ Flower	○ Annual		
○ Transplant	○ Shrub	○ Tree	○ Biennial		
○ Cutting	○ Herb		○ Perennial		
○ Bulb	○ Fruit				

Supplier: _____   Date Bloomed: _____

Cost: _____   Fertilizer / Soil Amendment:_____

Date Sown:_____   Pests / Weeds Control:_____

Date Germinated: _____   Date of First Harvest:_____

Date Planted Out:_____

PLANTING INSTRUCTIONS	CARE INSTRUCTIONS	FERTILIZERS & EQUIPMENT

DATE	EVENT

DATE HARVESTED	QUANTITY	WEIGHT

DATE HARVESTED	QUANTITY	WEIGHT

NOTES

Plant Profile

Plant Name:_____

Date Planted: _____

Date Purchase: _____

Purchase at: _____

Price: _____

Rate: ☆ ☆ ☆ ☆ ☆

STARTED FROM	PLANT TYPE		LIFE CYCLE	SUNLIGHT	WATER
○ Seed	○ Vegatable	○ Flower	○ Annual		
○ Transplant	○ Shrub	○ Tree	○ Biennial		
○ Cutting	○ Herb		○ Perennial		
○ Bulb	○ Fruit				

Supplier: _____   Date Bloomed: _____

Cost: _____   Fertilizer / Soil Amendment:_____

Date Sown: _____   Pests / Weeds Control:_____

Date Germinated: _____   Date of First Harvest:_____

Date Planted Out: _____

PLANTING INSTRUCTIONS	CARE INSTRUCTIONS	FERTILIZERS & EQUIPMENT

DATE	EVENT

DATE HARVESTED	QUANTITY	WEIGHT

DATE HARVESTED	QUANTITY	WEIGHT

NOTES

Plant Profile

Plant Name:_____

Date Planted: _____

Date Purchase: _____

Purchase at: _____

Price: _____

Rate: ☆ ☆ ☆ ☆ ☆

STARTED FROM	PLANT TYPE		LIFE CYCLE	SUNLIGHT	WATER
○ Seed	○ Vegatable	○ Flower	○ Annual		
○ Transplant	○ Shrub	○ Tree	○ Biennial		
○ Cutting	○ Herb		○ Perennial		
○ Bulb	○ Fruit				

Supplier: _____ Date Bloomed: _____

Cost:_____ Fertilizer / Soil Amendment:_____

Date Sown:_____ Pests / Weeds Control:_____

Date Germinated: _____ Date of First Harvest:_____

Date Planted Out:_____

PLANTING INSTRUCTIONS	CARE INSTRUCTIONS	FERTILIZERS & EQUIPMENT

DATE	EVENT

DATE HARVESTED	QUANTITY	WEIGHT

DATE HARVESTED	QUANTITY	WEIGHT

NOTES

Plant Profile

Plant Name:_____

Date Planted: _____

Date Purchase: _____

Purchase at: _____

Price: _____

Rate: ☆ ☆ ☆ ☆ ☆

STARTED FROM	PLANT TYPE		LIFE CYCLE	SUNLIGHT	WATER
○ Seed	○ Vegatable	○ Flower	○ Annual		
○ Transplant	○ Shrub	○ Tree	○ Biennial		
○ Cutting	○ Herb		○ Perennial		
○ Bulb	○ Fruit				

Supplier: _____

Cost: _____

Date Sown:_____

Date Germinated: _____

Date Planted Out: _____

Date Bloomed: _____

Fertilizer / Soil Amendment:_____

Pests / Weeds Control:_____

Date of First Harvest:_____

PLANTING INSTRUCTIONS	CARE INSTRUCTIONS	FERTILIZERS & EQUIPMENT

DATE	EVENT

DATE HARVESTED	QUANTITY	WEIGHT

DATE HARVESTED	QUANTITY	WEIGHT

NOTES

Plant Profile

Plant Name:_____

Date Planted: _____

Date Purchase: _____

Purchase at: _____

Price: _____

Rate: ☆ ☆ ☆ ☆ ☆

STARTED FROM	PLANT TYPE		LIFE CYCLE	SUNLIGHT	WATER
○ Seed	○ Vegatable	○ Flower	○ Annual	○ ☁	○ 💧
○ Transplant	○ Shrub	○ Tree	○ Biennial	○ ⛅	○ 💧💧
○ Cutting	○ Herb		○ Perennial	○ ☀	○ 💧💧💧
○ Bulb	○ Fruit				

Supplier: _____   Date Bloomed: _____

Cost: _____   Fertilizer / Soil Amendment: _____

Date Sown: _____   Pests / Weeds Control: _____

Date Germinated: _____   Date of First Harvest: _____

Date Planted Out: _____

PLANTING INSTRUCTIONS	CARE INSTRUCTIONS	FERTILIZERS & EQUIPMENT

DATE	EVENT

DATE HARVESTED	QUANTITY	WEIGHT

DATE HARVESTED	QUANTITY	WEIGHT

NOTES

Plant Profile

Plant Name:_____

Date Planted: _____

Date Purchase: _____

Purchase at: _____

Price: _____

Rate: ☆ ☆ ☆ ☆ ☆

STARTED FROM	PLANT TYPE		LIFE CYCLE	SUNLIGHT	WATER
○ Seed	○ Vegatable	○ Flower	○ Annual		
○ Transplant	○ Shrub	○ Tree	○ Biennial		
○ Cutting	○ Herb		○ Perennial		
○ Bulb	○ Fruit				

Supplier: _____ Date Bloomed: _____

Cost: _____ Fertilizer / Soil Amendment:_____

Date Sown:_____ Pests / Weeds Control:_____

Date Germinated: _____ Date of First Harvest:_____

Date Planted Out: _____

PLANTING INSTRUCTIONS	CARE INSTRUCTIONS	FERTILIZERS & EQUIPMENT

DATE	EVENT

DATE HARVESTED	QUANTITY	WEIGHT

DATE HARVESTED	QUANTITY	WEIGHT

NOTES

Plant Profile

Plant Name:_____

Date Planted: _____

Date Purchase: _____

Purchase at: _____

Price: _____

Rate: ☆ ☆ ☆ ☆ ☆

STARTED FROM	PLANT TYPE		LIFE CYCLE	SUNLIGHT	WATER
○ Seed	○ Vegatable	○ Flower	○ Annual		
○ Transplant	○ Shrub	○ Tree	○ Biennial		
○ Cutting	○ Herb		○ Perennial		
○ Bulb	○ Fruit				

Supplier: _____   Date Bloomed: _____

Cost: _____   Fertilizer / Soil Amendment:_____

Date Sown: _____   Pests / Weeds Control: _____

Date Germinated: _____   Date of First Harvest: _____

Date Planted Out:_____

PLANTING INSTRUCTIONS	CARE INSTRUCTIONS	FERTILIZERS & EQUIPMENT

DATE	EVENT

DATE HARVESTED	QUANTITY	WEIGHT

DATE HARVESTED	QUANTITY	WEIGHT

NOTES

Plant Profile

Plant Name:_____

Date Planted: _____

Date Purchase: _____

Purchase at: _____

Price: _____

Rate: ☆ ☆ ☆ ☆ ☆

STARTED FROM	PLANT TYPE		LIFE CYCLE	SUNLIGHT	WATER
○ Seed	○ Vegatable	○ Flower	○ Annual		
○ Transplant	○ Shrub	○ Tree	○ Biennial		
○ Cutting	○ Herb		○ Perennial		
○ Bulb	○ Fruit				

Supplier: _____   Date Bloomed: _____

Cost: _____   Fertilizer / Soil Amendment:_____

Date Sown: _____   Pests / Weeds Control:_____

Date Germinated: _____   Date of First Harvest:_____

Date Planted Out: _____

PLANTING INSTRUCTIONS	CARE INSTRUCTIONS	FERTILIZERS & EQUIPMENT

DATE	EVENT

DATE HARVESTED	QUANTITY	WEIGHT

DATE HARVESTED	QUANTITY	WEIGHT

NOTES

Plant Profile

Plant Name:_____

Date Planted: _____

Date Purchase: _____

Purchase at: _____

Price: _____

Rate: ☆☆☆☆☆

STARTED FROM	PLANT TYPE		LIFE CYCLE	SUNLIGHT	WATER
○ Seed	○ Vegatable	○ Flower	○ Annual		
○ Transplant	○ Shrub	○ Tree	○ Biennial		
○ Cutting	○ Herb		○ Perennial		
○ Bulb	○ Fruit				

Supplier: _____   Date Bloomed: _____

Cost: _____   Fertilizer / Soil Amendment:_____

Date Sown: _____   Pests / Weeds Control:_____

Date Germinated: _____   Date of First Harvest:_____

Date Planted Out:_____

PLANTING INSTRUCTIONS	CARE INSTRUCTIONS	FERTILIZERS & EQUIPMENT

DATE	EVENT

DATE HARVESTED	QUANTITY	WEIGHT

DATE HARVESTED	QUANTITY	WEIGHT

NOTES

Plant Profile

Plant Name:_____

Date Planted: _____

Date Purchase: _____

Purchase at: _____

Price: _____

Rate: ☆ ☆ ☆ ☆ ☆

STARTED FROM	PLANT TYPE		LIFE CYCLE	SUNLIGHT	WATER
○ Seed	○ Vegatable	○ Flower	○ Annual	○ ☁	○ 💧
○ Transplant	○ Shrub	○ Tree	○ Biennial	○ ⛅	○ 💧💧
○ Cutting	○ Herb		○ Perennial	○ ☀	○ 💧💧💧
○ Bulb	○ Fruit				

Supplier: _____   Date Bloomed: _____

Cost: _____   Fertilizer / Soil Amendment:_____

Date Sown: _____   Pests / Weeds Control:_____

Date Germinated: _____   Date of First Harvest:_____

Date Planted Out: _____

PLANTING INSTRUCTIONS	CARE INSTRUCTIONS	FERTILIZERS & EQUIPMENT

DATE	EVENT

DATE HARVESTED	QUANTITY	WEIGHT

DATE HARVESTED	QUANTITY	WEIGHT

NOTES

Plant Profile

Plant Name:_____

Date Planted: _____

Date Purchase: _____

Purchase at: _____

Price:_____

Rate: ☆ ☆ ☆ ☆ ☆

STARTED FROM	PLANT TYPE		LIFE CYCLE	SUNLIGHT	WATER
○ Seed	○ Vegatable	○ Flower	○ Annual		
○ Transplant	○ Shrub	○ Tree	○ Biennial		
○ Cutting	○ Herb		○ Perennial		
○ Bulb	○ Fruit				

Supplier: _____

Cost: _____

Date Sown: _____

Date Germinated: _____

Date Planted Out:_____

Date Bloomed: _____

Fertilizer / Soil Amendment:_____

Pests / Weeds Control:_____

Date of First Harvest:_____

PLANTING INSTRUCTIONS	CARE INSTRUCTIONS	FERTILIZERS & EQUIPMENT

DATE	EVENT

DATE HARVESTED	QUANTITY	WEIGHT

DATE HARVESTED	QUANTITY	WEIGHT

NOTES

Plant Profile

Plant Name:_____

Date Planted: _____

Date Purchase: _____

Purchase at: _____

Price: _____

Rate: ☆ ☆ ☆ ☆ ☆

STARTED FROM	PLANT TYPE		LIFE CYCLE	SUNLIGHT	WATER
○ Seed	○ Vegatable	○ Flower	○ Annual		
○ Transplant	○ Shrub	○ Tree	○ Biennial		
○ Cutting	○ Herb		○ Perennial		
○ Bulb	○ Fruit				

Supplier: _____   Date Bloomed: _____

Cost: _____   Fertilizer / Soil Amendment:_____

Date Sown: _____   Pests / Weeds Control:_____

Date Germinated: _____   Date of First Harvest:_____

Date Planted Out: _____

PLANTING INSTRUCTIONS	CARE INSTRUCTIONS	FERTILIZERS & EQUIPMENT

DATE	EVENT

DATE HARVESTED	QUANTITY	WEIGHT

DATE HARVESTED	QUANTITY	WEIGHT

NOTES

Plant Profile

Plant Name:_____

Date Planted: _____

Date Purchase: _____

Purchase at: _____

Price: _____

Rate: ☆ ☆ ☆ ☆ ☆

STARTED FROM	PLANT TYPE		LIFE CYCLE	SUNLIGHT	WATER
○ Seed	○ Vegatable	○ Flower	○ Annual		
○ Transplant	○ Shrub	○ Tree	○ Biennial		
○ Cutting	○ Herb		○ Perennial		
○ Bulb	○ Fruit				

Supplier: _____   Date Bloomed: _____

Cost: _____   Fertilizer / Soil Amendment:_____

Date Sown:_____   Pests / Weeds Control:_____

Date Germinated: _____   Date of First Harvest:_____

Date Planted Out: _____

PLANTING INSTRUCTIONS	CARE INSTRUCTIONS	FERTILIZERS & EQUIPMENT

DATE	EVENT

DATE HARVESTED	QUANTITY	WEIGHT

DATE HARVESTED	QUANTITY	WEIGHT

NOTES

For more Maky Publishing books visit our Amazon Store
and follow us on our social media accounts for updates!

Amazon

YouTube

Facebook

Instagram

Made in the USA
Las Vegas, NV
11 April 2023

70456564R00085